Pebble® Plus

Comida sana con MiPirámide/Healthy Eating with MyPyramid

El grupo de las verduras/The Vegetable Group

por/by Mari C. Schuh

Traducción/Translation: Dr. Martín Luis Guzmán Ferrer
Editor Consultor/Consulting Editor: Dra. Gail Saunders-Smith

Consultor/Consultant: Barbara J. Rolls, PhD
Guthrie Chair in Nutrition
The Pennsylvania State University
University Park, Pennsylvania

Capstone press®
Mankato, Minnesota

Pebble Plus is published by Capstone Press,
151 Good Counsel Drive, P.O. Box 669, Mankato, Minnesota 56002.
www.capstonepress.com

1 2 3 4 5 6 11 10 09 08 07 06

Library of Congress Cataloging-in-Publication Data
Schuh, Mari C., 1975–
    [Vegetable group. English & Spanish]
    El grupo de las verduras/de Mari C. Schuh = The vegetable group/by Mari C. Schuh.
    p. cm.—(Comida sana con MiPirámide = Healthy eating with MyPyramid)
    title: Vegetable group.
    Includes index.
    Parallel text in English and Spanish.
    ISBN-13: 978-0-7368-6672-9 (hardcover)
    ISBN-10: 0-7368-6672-8 (hardcover)
    1. Vegetables—Juvenile literature. 2. Nutrition—Juvenile literature. I. Title: Vegetable group. II. Title.
TX557.S3818 2007
641.3'5—dc22   2005037342

Summary: Simple text and photographs present the vegetable group, the foods in this group,
    and examples of healthy eating choices—in both English and Spanish.

Credits
Katy Kudela, bilingual editor; Eida del Risco, Spanish copy editor; Jennifer Bergstrom, designer;
    Kelly Garvin, photo researcher; Stacy Foster and Michelle Biedscheid, photo shoot coordinators

Photo Credits
BananaStock Ltd., 1; Capstone Press/Karon Dubke, cover, 5, 9, 11, 13, 15, 16–17, 18–19, 21, 22 (all);
Corbis/Andreas von Einsiedel/Elizabeth Whiting & Associates, 15 (background), 19 (background); Corbis/
Ariel Skelley, 6–7; Getty Images Inc./Patti McConville, 5 (background), 21 (background); U.S. Department
of Agriculture, 8, 9 (inset)

**Information in this book supports the U.S. Department of Agriculture's MyPyramid for Kids
food guidance system found at http://www.MyPyramid.gov/kids. Food amounts listed in this
book are based on an 1,800-calorie food plan.**

**The U.S. Department of Agriculture (USDA) does not endorse any products, services,
or organizations.**

Note to Parents and Teachers

The Comida sana con MiPirámide/Healthy Eating with MyPyramid set supports
national science standards related to nutrition and physical health. This book describes
the vegetable group in both English and Spanish. The images support early readers in
understanding the text. The repetition of words and phrases helps early readers learn new
words. This book also introduces early readers to subject-specific vocabulary words, which
are defined in the Glossary section. Early readers may need assistance to read some words
and to use the Table of Contents, Glossary, Internet Sites, and Index sections of the book.

Table of Contents

Tabla de contenidos

Vegetables

How many vegetables
have you eaten today?

Las verduras

¿Cuántas verduras
has comido hoy?

Did you know that vegetables
come from plants?
Vegetables help keep you
healthy and strong.

¿Sabías que las verduras
vienen de las plantas?
Las verduras te ayudan
a estar sano y fuerte.

MyPyramid for Kids

MyPyramid teaches you how much to eat from each food group. Vegetables are one food group in MyPyramid.

MiPirámide para niños

MiPirámide te enseña cuánto debes comer de cada uno de los grupos de alimentos. El grupo de las verduras es parte de MiPirámide.

MyPyramid For Kids
Eat Right. Exercise. Have Fun.

To learn more about healthy eating, go to this web site:
www.MyPyramid.gov/kids
Ask an adult for help.

Para saber más sobre comida sana, ve a este sitio de Internet:
www.MyPyramid.gov/kids
Pídele a un adulto que te ayude.

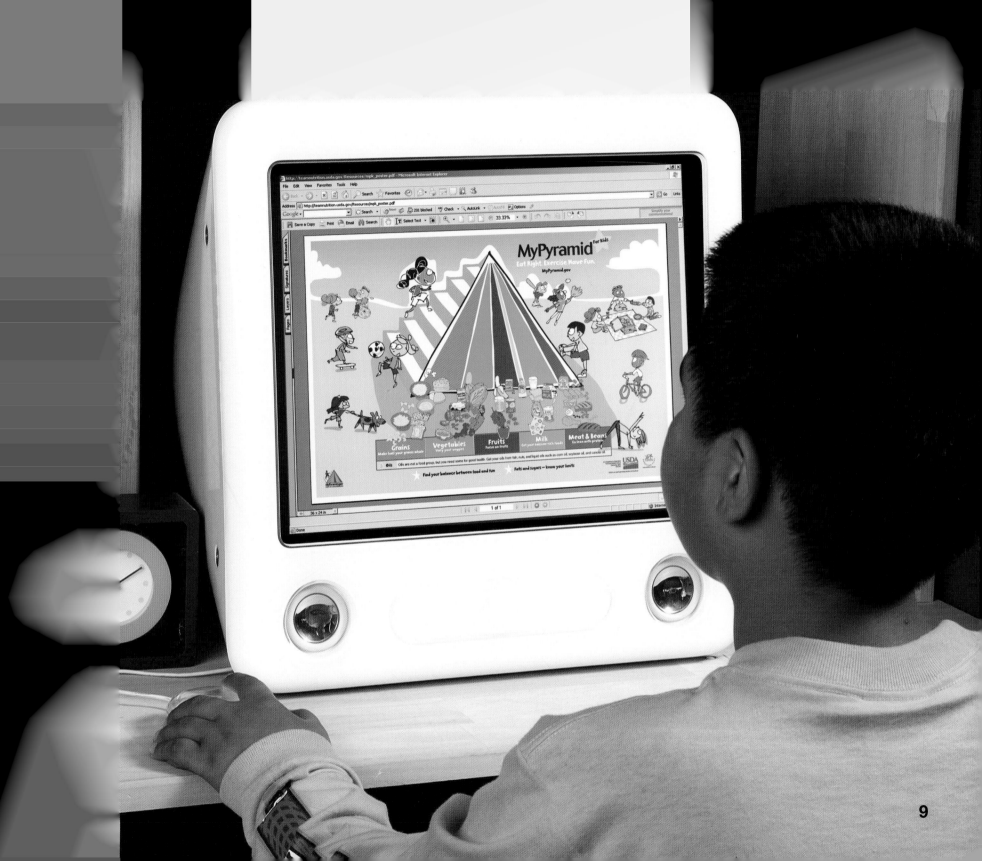

Kids should eat
at least 2½ cups
of vegetables every day.

Los niños deben comer por
lo menos 2½ tazas de
verduras todos los días.

Enjoying Vegetables

Cucumbers, carrots, cabbage.

There are all kinds of vegetables.

If you don't like one, try another.

Cómo disfrutar de las verduras

Pepinos, zanahorias, col.

Hay toda clase de verduras.

Si una no te gusta, prueba otra.

Yellow, red, green.

See how many colors you can eat.

Corn, tomatoes, and lettuce

are part of a healthy meal.

Amarillo, rojo, verde.

Mira cuántos colores puedes comerte.

El maíz, los tomates y la lechuga

son parte de una comida saludable.

Crunch, crunch, crunch.
Carrots and celery
make a fun snack.

Crunch, crunch, crunch.
Las zanahorias y el apio
resultan meriendas
muy divertidas.

You can make
a vegetable pizza.
Top it with peppers
and mushrooms.

Puedes hacer una
pizza de verduras.
Ponle pimientos y hongos.

Vegetables are part
of a healthy meal.
What are your
favorite vegetables?

Las verduras son parte
de una comida saludable.
¿Cuáles son tus verduras
preferidas?

How Much to Eat/Cuánto hay que comer

Kids need to eat at least 2½ cups of vegetables every day. To get 2½ cups, pick five of your favorite vegetables below.

La mayoría de los niños necesitan por lo menos 2½ tazas de verduras al día. Para completar 2½ tazas, escoge cinco de tus verduras preferidas entre las siguientes.

Pick five of your favorite vegetables to eat today!

¡Escoge cinco de tus verduras preferidas y cómetelas hoy!

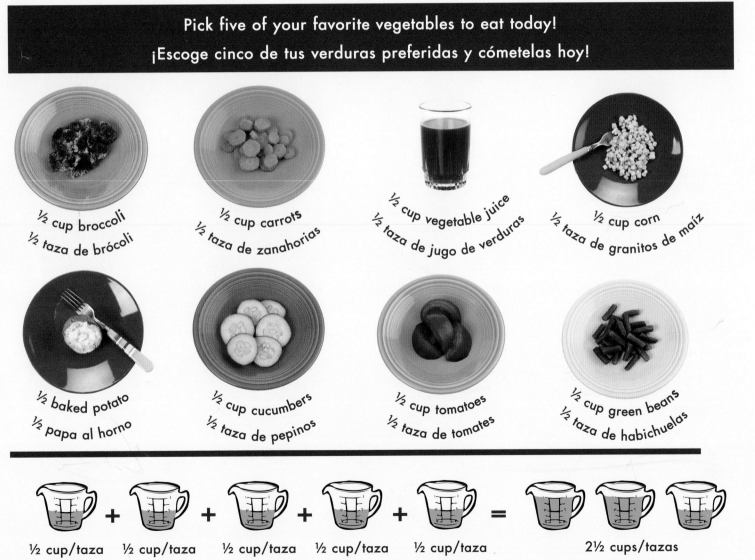

½ cup broccoli
½ taza de brócoli

½ cup carrots
½ taza de zanahorias

½ cup vegetable juice
½ taza de jugo de verduras

½ cup corn
½ taza de granitos de maíz

½ baked potato
½ papa al horno

½ cup cucumbers
½ taza de pepinos

½ cup tomatoes
½ taza de tomates

½ cup green beans
½ taza de habichuelas

½ cup/taza   ½ cup/taza   ½ cup/taza   ½ cup/taza   ½ cup/taza   =   2½ cups/tazas

Glossary

MyPyramid—a food plan that helps kids make healthy food choices and reminds kids to be active; MyPyramid was created by the U.S. Department of Agriculture.

snack—a small amount of food people eat when they are hungry between meals

vegetable—a part of a plant that people eat; vegetables come from many parts of a plant.

Glosario

la merienda—cantidad pequeña de comida que las personas toman entre comidas cuando tienen hambre

MiPirámide—plan de alimentos que ayuda a los chicos a escoger comidas saludables y a mantenerse activos; MiPirámide fue creada por el Departamento de Agricultura de los Estados Unidos.

las verduras—parte de la planta que se come; las verduras vienen de diversas partes de las plantas.

Index

Internet Sites

FactHound offers a safe, fun way to find Internet sites related to this book. All of the sites on FactHound have been researched by our staff.

Here's how:

1. Visit *www.facthound.com*

2. Choose your grade level.

3. Type in this book ID **0736866728** for age-appropriate sites. You may also browse subjects by clicking on letters, or by clicking on pictures and words.

4. Click on the **Fetch It** button.

FactHound will fetch the best sites for you!

Índice

Sitios de Internet

FactHound proporciona una manera divertida y segura de encontrar sitios de Internet relacionados con este libro. Nuestro personal ha investigado todos los sitios de FactHound. Es posible que los sitios no estén en español.

Se hace así:

1. Visita *www.facthound.com*

2. Elige tu grado escolar.

3. Introduce este código especial **0736866728** para ver sitios apropiados según tu edad, o usa una palabra relacionada con este libro para hacer una búsqueda general.

4. Haz clic en el botón **Fetch It**.

¡FactHound buscará los mejores sitios para ti!